A Penelope Pewter

MW00441950

bride

N o t e b o o k

Bride:

Wedding Date:

Special Note:

www.InspirationalWares.com

Goals:

- [ ]
- [ ]
- [ ]
- [ ]
- [ ]
- [ ]
- [ ]
- [ ]
- [ ]
- [ ]

Accomplishments:

- ○
- ○
- ○
- ○
- ○
- ○
- ○
- ○
- ○
- ○

Habit Tracker	1	2	3	4	5	6	7	8	9	10

Appointments & Special Dates:

Date:

Date:

Date:

Date:

Date:

Date:

Date:

Date:

Date:

Date:

Date:

Date:

Date:

Date:

Date:

Date:

Date:

Date:

Date:

Date:

Date:

Date:

Date:

Date:

Date:

Date:

Date:

Date:

Date:

Date:

Date:

Date:

Date:

Date:

Date:

Date:

Date:

Date:

Date:

Date:

Date:

Date:

Date:

Date:

Date:

Date:

Date:

Date:

Date:

Date:

Date:

For more amazing journals and adult coloring books from Penelope Pewter, visit:
Amazon.com
CreateSpace.com
RWSquaredMedia.Wordpress.com

She Believed She Could
So She Did Adult Coloring Book
with Inspirational Quotes

The Be A Pineapple Adult
Coloring Book

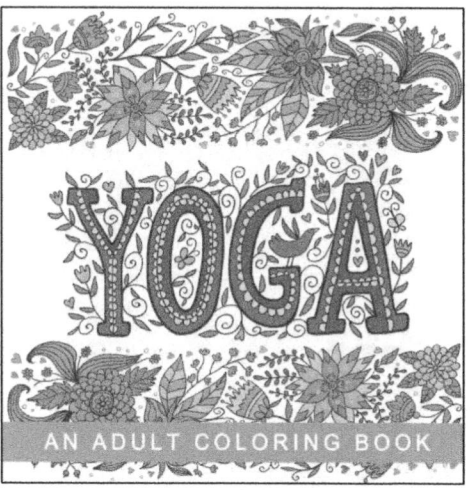

YOGA
An Adult Coloring Book

The Adult Coloring Book for
Coffee Lovers

InspirationalWares.com

Funny & inspirational calendars, posters, coffee mugs and more!

30010117R00064

Made in the USA
Middletown, DE
24 December 2018